20TH CENTURY ART
ART
1900-10
NEW WAYS OF SEEING

Please visit our web site at: www.garethstevens.com
For a frcc color catalog describing Gareth Stevens' list of high-quality books
and multimedia programs, call 1-800-542-2595 (USA) or 1-800-461-9120 (Canada).
Gareth Stevens Publishing's Fax: (414) 332-3567.

Library of Congress Cataloging-in-Publication Data available upon request from publisher.
Fax (414) 336-0157 for the attention of the Publishing Records Department.

ISBN 0-8368-2848-8

This North American edition first published in 2001 by
Gareth Stevens Publishing
A World Almanac Education Group Company
330 West Olive Street, Suite 100
Milwaukee, WI 53212 USA

Original edition © 2000 by David West Children's Books. First published in Great Britain in 2000 by
Heinemann Library, Halley Court, Jordan Hill, Oxford OX2 8EJ, a division of Reed Educational and
Professional Publishing Limited. This U.S. edition © 2001 by Gareth Stevens, Inc. Additional end
matter © 2001 by Gareth Stevens, Inc.

Picture Research: Brooks Krikler Research
Picture Editor: Carlotta Cooper
Gareth Stevens Editor: Dorothy L. Gibbs

Photo Credits:
Abbreviations: (t) top, (m) middle, (b) bottom, (l) left, (r) right

AKG London: pages 4, 9(t), 12(l), 13(r), 14(bl), 17(t), 18(l), 19(b), 20(b), 21(l), 22(l), 24(t), 25, 28(t).
AKG London © ADAGP, Paris, and DACS, London, 2000: page 27.
AKG London © DACS 2000: page 20(t).
Bridgeman Art Library: pages 5(t), 6(both), 7(t), 8, 9(br), 10(both), 11(t), 13(l), 14(t, br), 15, 21(r),
    22(r), 28(b), 29(t).
Bridgeman Art Library © ADAGP, Paris, and DACS, London, 2000: pages 26(b), 29(b).
Bridgeman Art Library © Succession H. Matisse/DACS 2000: page 19(t).
Bridgeman Art Library/Lauros-Giraudon: page 5(b).
Bridgeman Art Library/Roger Violett, Paris: page 24(b).
Mary Evans Picture Library: pages 3, 16(both).
J. Lathion © Munch Museum/munch-ellingsen Group, BONO, Oslo, and DACS, London, 2000:
    page 12(r).
MOMA © Succession Picasso/DACS 2000: page 23.
Tate Publishing © ADAGP, Paris, and DACS, London, 2000: cover, page 17(b).

Printed in the United States of America

1 2 3 4 5 6 7 8 9 05 04 03 02 01

20TH CENTURY ART

1900-10

NEW WAYS OF SEEING

Jackie Gaff

Gareth Stevens Publishing
A WORLD ALMANAC EDUCATION GROUP COMPANY

CONTENTS

Spanish-born Pablo Picasso (1881–1973) was probably the most famous artist of the 20th century. Many believe he was also the greatest. Picasso visited Paris for the first time in 1900. He was just nineteen years old, and few people outside his homeland had ever heard of him, when one of his paintings was chosen for the Spanish pavilion at the Paris World's Fair.

CHANGING PERSPECTIVES

Western art changed more in the first decade of the 20th century than at any time in the previous five centuries. Avant-garde painters abandoned naturalistic color and perspective and stopped painting the world as it appears to our eyes. What artists saw became less important than expressing their personal inner visions.

Most of the new ideas in Western art were born in France. Paris had long been the center of the art world. Modern art began there in the 19th century, when a group of young painters, now called Impressionists, took the first steps to overthrow five hundred years of tradition. Impressionist paintings are now among the world's best loved. Back in 1874, however, "impressionist" was the horrified response of an art critic to the radical new style of Frenchman Claude Monet (1840–1926).

In 1900, millions of people visited the Paris World's Fair, where thousands of paintings and sculptures from all over the world were shown in new, specially constructed art galleries.

5

Monet and other Impressionists were fascinated by modern technology, including the 19th century's biggest symbol of progress and speed — the steam engine!

LA GARE SAINT-LAZARE, *Claude Monet, 1877*

IMPRESSIONISM

In Monet's day, the accepted style of painting was an almost photographic depiction of reality. Such detail demanded a level of technical skill that took years of training to achieve, and a finished painting could take months to complete. Artists worked indoors in their studios, even to paint landscapes. The traditional subjects of their paintings were weighty, including religious and mythological scenes and historical events.

The invention of photography in the 1820s freed artists from the responsibility of reproducing reality in precise detail.

6

A MODERN WAY OF LIFE

Impressionists wanted to portray the bustling, turn-of-the-century society that was growing right outside their studios. They were influenced, too, by discoveries in optics, which is the science of light. Trying to capture the way human eyes perceive the flickering effects of natural light, these artists had to work rapidly, using quick, rough brushstrokes. As a result, their work looked sketchy and unfinished to 19th-century eyes.

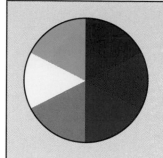

COLOR THEORIES
Scientists discovered that a color's brightness depends on the colors beside it. The vibrant Impressionist style came from using complementary colors, such as red with green, yellow with purple, or blue with orange.

In the 1880s, Australian artists Arthur Streeton (1867–1943) and Tom Roberts (1856–1931) began to use Impressionist techniques to portray the distinctive colors of the Australian landscape.

THE WALK (ARGENTEUIL)
CLAUDE MONET, c. 1872–1875

Impressionists were fascinated by the play of natural light flickering on surfaces. Their paintings seem to vibrate with color. Impressionist artists often worked outdoors, painting snapshotlike images of Parisians enjoying weekends in the country. New railways had brought the countryside within easy reach of city dwellers. Painting outdoors became possible with the invention, in the 1840s, of portable metal paint tubes.

SUMMER DROVING, *Arthur Streeton, 1891*

7

THE FRENCH IMPRESSIONISTS

Besides Monet, the leading Impressionists based in France included French artists Edgar Degas (1834–1917), Edouard Manet (1832–1883), Berthe Morisot (1841–1895), Camille Pissarro (1830–1903), and Auguste Renoir (1841–1919); American Mary Cassatt (1844–1926); and Englishman Alfred Sisley (1839–1899).

Later in life, Monet worked in his studio, creating a series of vast canvases of the water lily pond outside his house in Giverny, near Paris.

POINTILLISM

One of Impressionism's first spin-offs was the art style commonly known as Pointillism, from the French word *point*, which means "dot." Georges Seurat (1859–1891), the French artist who developed Pointillism in the 1880s, preferred to call it Divisionism.

Seurat's Pointillist paintings are meant to be viewed from a distance.

(Up close, you see tiny dots of pure color.)

A SUNDAY AFTERNOON ON THE ISLAND OF LA GRANDE JATTE
GEORGES SEURAT, c. 1884–1886

Wanting to create something more permanent than a "snapshot" impression of what the eye sees in a glance, Seurat composed his paintings carefully to achieve order, balance, and harmony.

Works such as *La Grande Jatte* have a feeling of monumental stillness and calm. Such attention to detail took time. Seurat worked in his studio on this particular painting for over a year.

8

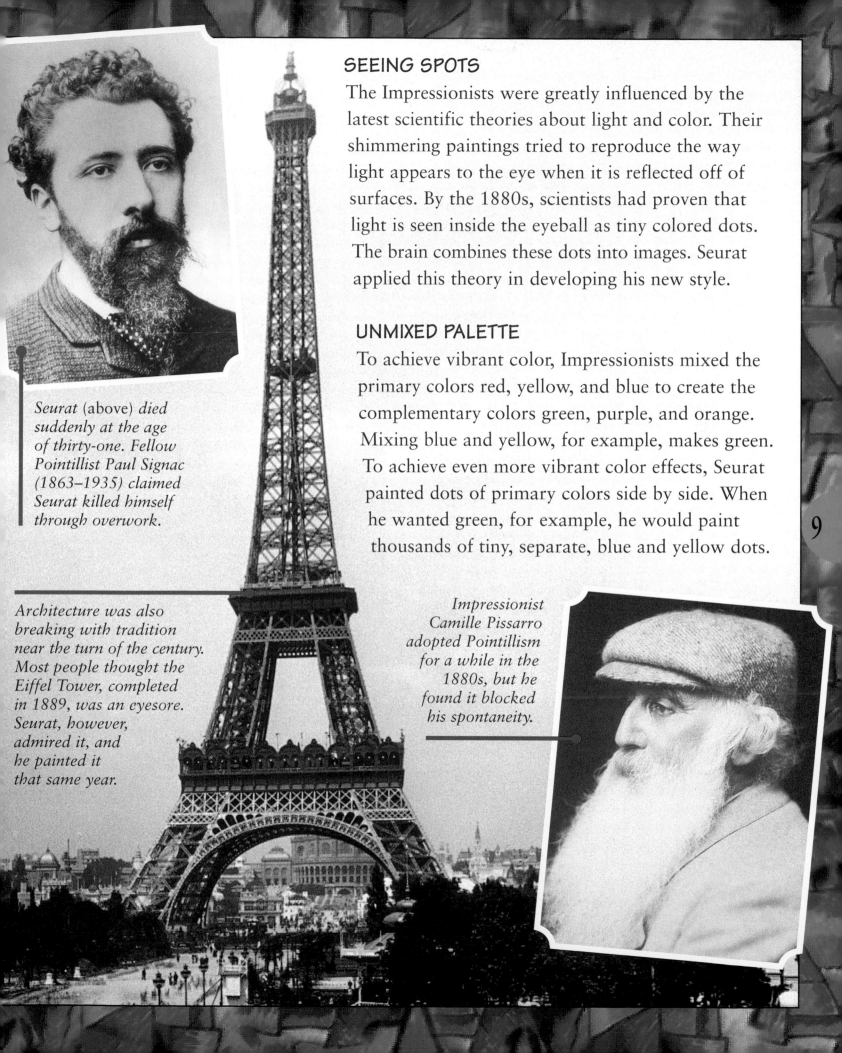

SEEING SPOTS

The Impressionists were greatly influenced by the latest scientific theories about light and color. Their shimmering paintings tried to reproduce the way light appears to the eye when it is reflected off of surfaces. By the 1880s, scientists had proven that light is seen inside the eyeball as tiny colored dots. The brain combines these dots into images. Seurat applied this theory in developing his new style.

UNMIXED PALETTE

To achieve vibrant color, Impressionists mixed the primary colors red, yellow, and blue to create the complementary colors green, purple, and orange. Mixing blue and yellow, for example, makes green. To achieve even more vibrant color effects, Seurat painted dots of primary colors side by side. When he wanted green, for example, he would paint thousands of tiny, separate, blue and yellow dots.

Seurat (above) *died suddenly at the age of thirty-one. Fellow Pointillist Paul Signac (1863–1935) claimed Seurat killed himself through overwork.*

Architecture was also breaking with tradition near the turn of the century. Most people thought the Eiffel Tower, completed in 1889, was an eyesore. Seurat, however, admired it, and he painted it that same year.

Impressionist Camille Pissarro adopted Pointillism for a while in the 1880s, but he found it blocked his spontaneity.

9

VINCENT VAN GOGH

After artists had gone about as far as they could in translating the science of light into the poetry of painting, the shift away from naturalistic color met with an increasing focus on emotions.

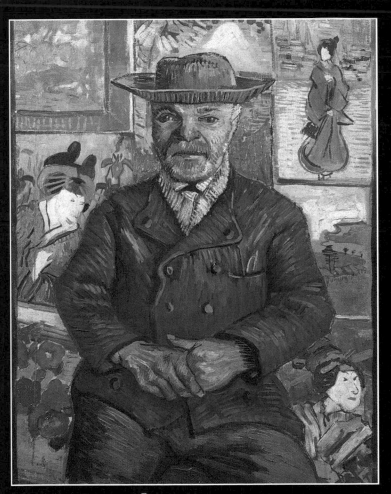

PÈRE TANGUY
VINCENT VAN GOGH, 1887

Van Gogh admired the expressive qualities and strong, flat colors of Japanese prints like the ones he copied in the background of this portrait. He also appreciated that Japanese artists did not try to reproduce exactly what they saw.

WOODBLOCK PRINT, Kitagawa Utamaro (1753–1806), c. 1797

GOING JAPANESE
Japanese woodblock prints, first seen in Europe in the 1850s, had a great influence on avant-garde Western art. Their simplified forms, flat colors, unusual composition, and flattened perspective were new to Western eyes.

PAINTING FROM THE HEART
Dutch painter Vincent van Gogh (1853–1890) believed that Impressionism could not portray feelings. By the end of his short life, van Gogh had found a personal style of painting that expressed strong emotions, such as joy, hope, fear, and sorrow.

WHERE DO WE COME FROM? WHAT ARE WE? WHERE ARE WE GOING?
PAUL GAUGUIN, 1897

In 1895, Paul Gauguin turned his back on Western civilization and moved to the South Pacific, where he hoped to cultivate his art into "something primitive and wild."

Gauguin wanted to paint the inner world of the imagination and the soul. In *Where Do We Come From?*, he portrayed the cycle of life from infancy to old age.

Near the end of his life, van Gogh was tormented by intense depression that drove him to suicide at the age of thirty-seven. Van Gogh's life has been the subject of many books and films. In the 1956 film Lust for Life, *van Gogh was played by actor Kirk Douglas* (left) *and Gauguin by Anthony Quinn* (right).

THE ART OF PASSION

Van Gogh used paint thickly, laying it on the canvas with broad, bold brushstrokes. To van Gogh, colors represented feelings. Yellow, for example, the color of sunshine, meant life, hope, and happiness. About his painting *The Night Café* (1888), van Gogh said, "I have tried to express the terrible passions of humanity by means of red and green."

A PASSION FOR ART

Van Gogh collaborated briefly with French artist Paul Gauguin (1848–1903). Their artistic differences, however, led to a violent quarrel on Christmas Eve, in 1888, after which van Gogh cut off his own earlobe.

EXPRESSIONISM

Although its foundations were laid in the 1880s, Expressionism, as we know it, did not gather enough strength to be labeled an art movement until the early 1900s. Vincent van Gogh and Norwegian Edvard Munch (1863–1944) were the artists who started the movement. Munch's *The Cry* is one of the world's most famous paintings.

THE CRY
EDVARD MUNCH, 1893

Describing the birth of his most famous painting, Munch said, "I was tired and ill. I stood looking out across the fjord. The Sun was setting. The clouds were colored red — like blood. I felt as though a scream went through nature . . . The colors were screaming."

After a nervous breakdown in 1908, Munch abandoned the anguished imagery of his earlier work.

EMOTIONAL INTENSITY

As its name suggests, Expressionism was all about expressing inner feelings. It was an anti-naturalistic style that used vigorous brushstrokes and exaggerated or distorted shapes and colors to create the most intense emotional storms possible. Unlike van Gogh, who created joyful paintings as well as sad ones, Munch had an artistic view of the world that was, for many years, a long, waking nightmare.

One of Munch's inspirations for The Cry *was an Incan mummy that he saw at the Paris World's Fair in 1889. For Munch, this mummy was the embodiment of fear and panic. Gauguin was also fascinated by the mummy and used it as an image of death in some of his paintings.*

FREUDIAN ANALYSIS

In developing his theories on the workings of the human mind, Austrian psychoanalyst Sigmund Freud (1856–1939) concluded that much of our behavior is shaped by the unconscious, the part of our minds that contains memories, thoughts, and feelings of which we are unaware. Although Freud's theories were not widely known until well into the 20th century, painters such as Edvard Munch were already expressing them artistically in the 1890s.

13

Freud argued that our dreams can contain clues to our unconscious.

MIRROR OF THE SOUL

Edvard Munch had a tragic childhood. After his mother and his older sister died of tuberculosis, his father, driven almost insane with grief, developed a religious obsession that sometimes erupted in violence. Munch wrote, "For as long as I can remember I have suffered from a deep feeling of anxiety which I have tried to express in my art." Until his own breakdown in 1908, his paintings were as tortured as his life. He exposed his innermost feelings of love, sickness, death, and the fear and loneliness so vividly expressed in the swirling, unnatural shapes and colors of *The Cry*.

SYMBOLISM

Because the "isms" of art history are often invented by art critics well after the development of a new style, they can include artists whose work appears puzzlingly different. The Symbolism movement of the late 19th century included one of the most eclectic artistic groupings. Symbolist art varied wildly in both style and subject.

MATERIAL WORLD

Symbolism was a reaction to the naturalism of the Impressionists and to the greedy materialism of modern industrial life. Gauguin was a leading Symbolist, and Munch is often described as one. Other Symbolists included Frenchmen Gustave Moreau (1826–1898) and Odilon Redon (1840–1916), Dutchman Jan Toorop (1858–1928), and Austrian Gustav Klimt (1862–1918). Instead of depicting the real world, these artists drew upon their ideas, emotions, imaginations, and dreams. Their subjects were exotic and mystical.

Gustav Klimt was a large man with an intense passion for life and love. Many of his contemporaries criticized Klimt's work as corrupt and decadent.

THE CYCLOPS, *Odilon Redon, 1898–1900*

Redon was described by one critic as the "prince of mysterious dreams." In Greek mythology, the giant one-eyed Cyclops was hopelessly in love with the nymph Galatea.

ART NOUVEAU

In the 1890s and early 1900s, the curling, twisting lines and stylized natural imagery of art nouveau were at the height of their popularity in architecture and the decorative arts. The influence of art nouveau can be seen in the swirling shapes of Munch's *The Cry* and Klimt's *The Kiss.*

This art nouveau lampshade was designed by American Louis Comfort Tiffany (1848–1933).

14

THE KISS
GUSTAV KLIMT, 1907–1908

Klimt's work spanned Symbolism and art nouveau. His painting *The Kiss* is one of the world's most luxurious and decorative celebrations of desire. In it, a man and a woman kneel and kiss in a field of flowers, lost in their own golden dream of love.

Klimt, who had trained as an applied artist, loved gold leaf and rich patterns. In the 1900s, he created glittering mosaic murals for the Vienna Workshops, a group of artists and craftworkers who created the Austrian version of art nouveau.

FAUVISM

In 1905, the rumblings of an artistic revolution finally erupted into the first major avant-garde art movement of the 20th century — Fauvism.

This review of a scandalous Fauvist exhibition appeared in the November 4, 1905, issue of the French weekly magazine L'Illustration.

THE WILD ONES

If art critics had scorned the Impressionists back in the 1870s, it was nothing compared to their reaction to Fauvists. Some described Fauvists as "invertebrates" and "incoherents." When art critic Louis Vauxcelles (*b.* 1870; *d.* unknown) jokingly exclaimed that they painted like "wild beasts," or *fauves*, the name stuck.

EXPLODING COLOR

What people found so shocking about Fauvism was the savagely unnatural use of color. The group's leader, Henri Matisse (1869–1954), for example, painted a portrait of his wife with a bright green streak down the center of her face.

16

THE MASTERPIECE, *Albert Guillaume, 1905*

PICTURE PALACES
France's official annual art exhibition was the Paris Salon. Dating back to the 17th century, it was a showcase for traditional painting and sculpture. People went there to admire conventional works of art, as shown *(left)* by an illustrator on the magazine *L'Illustration.* Salon des Indépendants, formed in 1884, and Salon d'Automne, founded in 1903, were two major annual exhibitions set up in opposition to the Salon. They showed modern art.

THE POOL OF LONDON
ANDRÉ DERAIN, 1906

Outrage at the first Fauvist exhibition was accompanied by instant fame in Parisian art circles, and art dealers subsequently offered contracts to several artists. In late 1905, avant-garde dealer Ambroise Vollard (c. 1867–1939) commissioned André Derain to visit London, where Derain created some of his best works. In *The Pool of London,* as in other Fauvist works, color, rather than the scene, was the subject of the painting. Derain wrote of Fauvism, "Colors became charges of dynamite . . . everything could be raised above the real."

While Impressionists had used bright colors to represent natural light, Fauvists freed color from reality. Their unnatural colors were bold, fierce, and often deliberately clashing.

SHORT BUT SWEET

The Fauvists all were French except Dutch-born Kees van Dongen (1877–1968). Besides Matisse, they included André Derain (1880–1954), Albert Marquet (1875–1947), Georges Rouault (1871–1958), and Maurice de Vlaminck (1876–1958). Fauvism, however, was short-lived. By 1907, its artists had gone separate ways — some to continue on alone, others to experiment with new styles.

PORTRAIT OF AMBROISE VOLLARD, *Paul Cézanne, 1899*

Gauguin, van Gogh, Derain, de Vlaminck, Picasso, Matisse, and Cézanne (1839–1906) all were among the avant-garde painters championed by art dealer Ambroise Vollard.

17

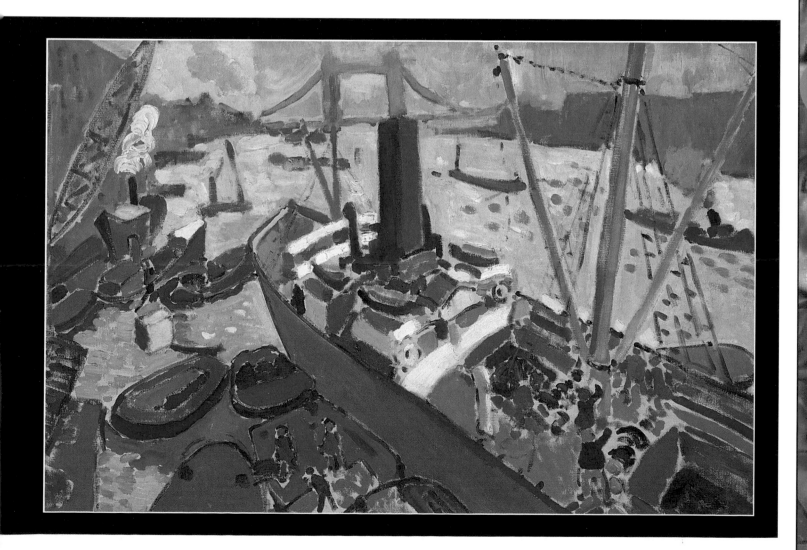

THE KING OF COLOR

Henri Matisse was a genius who enriched art in all kinds of ways, from color to composition. With works like *The Dance (II)*, Matisse helped shift the focus of composition from perspective and depth to the harmonious and expressive use of color.

DEPTH OF COLOR

In traditional art, perspective is used to make paintings that are like mirrors reflecting our eyes' three-dimensional view of the world around us. In 1908, Matisse wrote, "What I am after above all is expression . . . Expression to my way of thinking does not consist of the passion mirrored upon a human face . . . The whole arrangement of my pictures is expressive . . . Composition is the art of arranging in a decorative manner the various elements at a painter's disposal for the expression of his feelings."

Vaslav Nijinsky (1890–1950) was the star of the Russian Ballet.

DANCING TO A NEW TUNE
The Russian Ballet caused a sensation when it first performed in Paris in 1909. As with art, a revolution took place in dance, too. Believing that classical ballet technique was artificial and meaningless, pioneers of modern dance, such as the Russian Ballet, explored freedom of expression and movement.

THE DANCE (II)
HENRI MATISSE, 1910

Although he created designs for the Russian Ballet in 1920, Matisse is said to have preferred country dancing. The sardana, a circular country dance, is thought to have inspired *The Dance (II)*, a huge 13- by 8-foot (3.9- by 2.6-meter) mural commissioned for the Moscow home of Russian Sergei Shchukin (1854-1936), Matisse's biggest patron. Using just three colors, Matisse expressed all the wild abandon of dancing.

In 1905, at age thirty-six, Matisse was the oldest Fauvist — and the group's natural leader. The serious-looking Matisse was nicknamed "the Doctor."

18

MATISSE THE MASTER

One of the great masters of 20th-century art, Matisse experimented with color and composition throughout his long life. In his seventies and bedridden with illness, he began cutting out shapes from boldly painted sheets of paper. His assistants would move the cutouts around until Matisse was satisfied with the composition and balance of color. Some of his most brilliant works, such as *The Snail* (1953), were created this way in the last years of his life.

Writer and art collector Gertrude Stein (1874–1946) was a friend and generous patron to Matisse, Picasso, and other avant-garde artists. Wealthy collectors played a crucial role in supporting modern artists early in their careers.

NORTHERN EXPRESSIONISM

The term Expressionism was first seen in print, in 1911, describing a German avant-garde group founded in 1905, the same year the first Fauvist exhibition rocked Paris. Like the Fauvists, the northern European Expressionists distorted color and shape. Most Fauvist paintings, however, radiated a kind of joyful harmony. The Expressionist paintings were far more jagged and harsh.

Northern European Expressionists included Austrians Egon Schiele (1890–1918) and Oskar Kokoschka (1886–1980). Kokoschka, who was a playwright as well as a painter, created this poster for one of his own plays.

The new group of German avant-garde artists formed in Dresden. By 1911, however, the entire group had moved to Berlin, where the artistic and social scenes were far more vibrant — and decadent!

20

POSTER FOR MURDERER, HOPE OF WOMEN, *Oskar Kokoschka, 1909*

BUILDING "THE BRIDGE"

The Germans called themselves *Die Brücke,* which means "the bridge." Founding members of the group were Fritz Bleyl (1880–1966), Erich Heckel (1883–1970), Ernst Ludwig Kirchner (1880–1938), and Karl Schmidt-Rottluff (1884–1976). One of Die Brücke's goals was to escape the dominance of French culture. In 1912, Kirchner wrote, "We have a duty to separate ourselves from the French . . . it is time for an independent German art."

WOMEN IN ART

Although not widely known at the time of her death, Paula Modersohn-Becker (1876–1907) was one of the leading German artists of the 1900s, a time when it was still very hard for women to train or be accepted as artists, particularly among the avant-garde. Because her painting is less concerned with portraying reality than expressing inner feelings, she is often called an Expressionist.

SELF-PORTRAIT, *Paula Modersohn-Becker, 1900s*

SELF-PORTRAIT WITH MODEL
ERNST LUDWIG KIRCHNER, 1910 (*overpainted in 1926*)

Die Brücke artists wanted to express themselves "directly and passionately." Their main subject was their own way of life. Like many avant-garde artists of the period, they aimed for artistic and social freedom, leading bohemian lifestyles and deliberately scorning accepted codes of social behavior. Many of Kirchner's early paintings were set indoors in his studio, using himself and one of his many girlfriends as models. The model sitting on the bed in *Self-Portrait with Model* was called Dodo. She was the most important woman in Kirchner's life, and art, from 1909 to 1911.

LES DEMOISELLES D'AVIGNON

If traditional painting held a mirror up to reality, in 1907, Spanish artist Pablo Picasso (1881–1973) threw a stone at the mirror and shattered it. Even Picasso's friends were shocked by *Les Demoiselles d'Avignon*. One of them said that looking at it was like being forced to drink gasoline!

REVOLUTIONARY ART

Picasso's controversial painting was a guerrilla attack on the traditional treatment of form, the individual shapes in a work of art and the relationships between them. Instead of three-dimensional reality, he created two-dimensional, angular planes that resembled shattered glass.

AFRICAN INSPIRATION

In the 19th century, with European colonization of Africa at its height, a flood of plundered art objects appeared in European markets. Few people in Europe, including Picasso, knew anything about the ritual or tribal meanings of this art, but they responded to the energy and freedom of its distorted reality.

TRIBAL MASK from the African Congo

STRANGE BEAUTY

The distorted heads of the two women on the right-hand side of the painting were inspired by African masks. Picasso had seen African sculptures at a Paris museum and said they were "the most powerful and the most beautiful of all the products of the human imagination." In the end, however, Picasso hid *Les Demoiselles* away in a corner of his studio.

This photograph of Picasso was taken in 1904, the year he left Spain and settled in Paris.

22

LES DEMOISELLES D'AVIGNON
PABLO PICASSO, 1907

Picasso set out to shock people with his treatment of this painting's subject. Instead of art history's soft, submissive female forms, he portrayed anger and aggression. Instead of celebrating beauty, he flaunted ugliness.

The viewpoints in this painting are deliberately confusing. For example, Picasso has painted some of the women with their eyes facing straight forward but their noses in profile, facing sideways.

PAUL CÉZANNE

Picasso's chief inspiration for the shifting viewpoints in *Les Demoiselles d'Avignon* came from the paintings of the great French artist Paul Cézanne (1839–1906).

THE HEART OF THE MATTER

Cézanne began painting in the 1860s. He experimented with Impressionism for a while but soon decided that he wanted to do something more "solid and durable." The problem with Impressionism, he thought, was that it dealt with only the surface of nature. Cézanne wanted to expose the heart and the skeleton. In trying to do so, he developed a new approach to volume, which is the space a three-dimensional object appears to fill in a painting.

Cézanne was born in Aix-en-Provence in southern France. He studied law before moving to Paris to paint, when he was in his early twenties. In the 1880s, Cézanne returned to Provence and remained there until his death.

24

TRICKS OF THE TRADE

Techniques of perspective are used to create the illusion of three-dimensional space and depth on a flat surface. One technique is to draw lines extending into the distance so they meet on the horizon. In real life, the lines would be parallel. Another technique is to make distant objects smaller than close ones, even though in real life they are the same size.

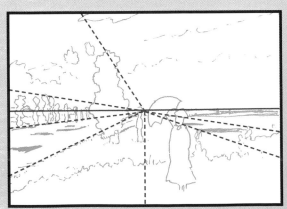

The place where lines of perspective meet is called the vanishing point.

A QUESTION OF PERSPECTIVE

Paintings are, of course, flat, two-dimensional objects. Artists use perspective to give the illusion of space and depth. In traditional art, perspective was based on a single, fixed viewpoint. As Cézanne struggled to get to the heart of nature, he found it impossible to maintain this fixed viewpoint. Whenever he blinked his eyes or moved his head, his view shifted.

A CHANGE OF VIEWPOINT

Cézanne built this shifting viewpoint into his later paintings, such as the scenes of Mont Sainte-Victoire. This technique is one reason many people now consider Cézanne the greatest artist of the 19th century and the most influential figure in the development of modern art.

MONT SAINTE-VICTOIRE
PAUL CÉZANNE, 1904–1905

This painting is one of more than ten oil paintings in which Cézanne tried to capture the essence, or heart, of a mountain near his home in Provence. *Mont* is the French word for "mountain." There are no perspective devices to lead our eyes toward the horizon in this landscape, as the trees do in Monet's *The Walk (Argenteuil)* on page 6. Instead, both the mountain and the fields and trees in front of it seem near and far away at the same time. Cézanne built his paintings with blocks of color, like the pieces of a mosaic, often showing objects from different angles at the same time.

25

This photograph of Mont Sainte-Victoire was taken from the road outside Cézanne's studio.

CUBISM

Inspired by Cézanne's unique style of painting, and jump-started by Picasso's outrageous *Les Demoiselles d'Avignon*, the revolutionary art movement known as Cubism exploded on the scene late in 1907. It was the joint creation of Picasso and his friend Georges Braque (1882–1963), a French artist.

The painting style of Georges Braque, who lived to the age of eighty-one, changed at different stages of his career. In the 1920s, his style became more fluid and less angular than his early Cubist works.

FAME AT LAST

Cézanne's work was not widely known until after 1895, when art dealer Ambroise Vollard gave him a one-man show in Paris. Among Cézanne's admirers was French artist Maurice Denis (1870–1943). In 1890, Denis had drawn attention to the contradiction of showing a three-dimensional scene on a two-dimensional surface. "Remember," Denis declared, "that a picture — before being a war horse or a nude woman . . . is essentially a flat surface covered with colors assembled in a certain order."

HOMAGE TO CÉZANNE, *Maurice Denis, 1900*

CREATIVE PARTNERSHIP

Picasso and Braque worked together so closely over the next few years that it is often hard to tell their paintings apart. Braque said they were "roped together like mountaineers." Together they achieved an entirely new way of looking at the world. The old idea of a single, fixed viewpoint was shattered. Picasso and Braque broke apart people, objects, and landscapes and painted them from several angles at once. The cubelike forms and geometric patterns that resulted gave rise to the term "Cubism." That term was coined by Louis Vauxcelles, the same art critic who had named Fauvism back in 1905.

HOUSES AT L'ESTAQUE
GEORGES BRAQUE, 1908

In 1908, Braque, who was an ardent admirer of Cézanne, visited L'Estaque in southern France. L'Estaque is the place Cézanne lived and worked in the 1870s.

In Braque's painting, the houses are cubes and triangles, much like children's building blocks. Some of their corners seem to jut out of the canvas. Others point into it.

CONSTANTIN BRANCUSI

By the late 1900s, sculpture, like painting, stood poised between the old world and the new. The most radical sculptor of the period, and one of the most respected and influential of all 20th-century artists, was Constantin Brancusi (1876–1957). Although born in Romania, Brancusi settled in France in 1904.

By 1900, Rodin had gained such respect that an entire pavilion was devoted to his sculptures at the World's Fair in Paris.

ACORN OF INDEPENDENCE

In Paris, Brancusi met the great French sculptor Auguste Rodin (1840–1917). Brancusi admired Rodin enormously, and Rodin's influence was evident in Brancusi's work. When Rodin offered to take Brancusi on as an assistant, however, Brancusi refused. "No other tree," he said, "can grow in the shadow of an oak."

SIMPLICITY OF FORM AND THE MEANING OF A KISS

By 1907, Brancusi had started to develop his own distinctive style. It was based on simplifying form to create universal truths — things so powerful that they speak to our deepest feelings. Brancusi created his first sculpture in this new style in about 1908. He called it *The Kiss*. Although it has the same title as Rodin's famous sculpture, the two works are centuries apart.

THE KISS, *Auguste Rodin, 1886*

CARVED IN STONE

Brancusi was a master stonecutter and helped revive the art of direct carving, which is making a sculpture by cutting directly into the material. In the 19th century, sculptors had modeled their work in clay or wax. To have something cast in bronze or carved in marble was expensive, and usually done only after the sculpture was paid for. Successful sculptors, such as Rodin, employed assistants to copy their work in stone, with the sculptor sometimes adding the finishing touches.

This photograph of Brancusi's studio shows one of his bird sculptures toward the back. "Why write [about my sculptures]," he said. "Why not just show the photographs?"

THE SIMPLE LIFE

Brancusi continued to refine and simplify his sculpture throughout his long life. His themes of creation, life, and death were monumental, but his subjects were as pared down as his style. Pure, egg-shaped heads symbolized dreaming and creation, and birds were elongated into teardrops, soaring upward through space and time.

THE KISS
Constantin Brancusi, *c.* 1908

Carved from a single block of stone, two lovers are locked in a kiss for eternity. Brancusi said his distinctive style was based on his feeling that "what is real is not the external form but the essence of things. Starting from this truth it is impossible for anyone to express anything essentially real by imitating its exterior surface." Brancusi made a series of versions of *The Kiss*. One of them, carved in 1909, was placed in the Parisian cemetery of Montparnasse, on the grave of a young girl who had committed suicide.

29

· T I M E   L I N E ·

	ART	WORLD EVENTS	DESIGN	THEATER & FILM	BOOKS & MUSIC
1900	•*Paris: art and sculpture of 29 nations exhibited at the World's Fair* •*Redon:* The Cyclops	•*China: Boxer Rebellion* •*U.K. Labour Party formed*	•*Paris design exhibition celebrates art nouveau*	•*Henrik Ibsen:* When We Dead Awaken •*Death of Oscar Wilde*	•*Freud:* The Interpretation of Dreams •*Puccini:* Tosca
1901	•*Picasso's Blue Period (to 1904)* •*Cézanne's one-man show at Vollard's Paris gallery*	•*Commonwealth of Australia proclaimed* •*U.S.: President McKinley shot*	•*Victor Horta: A L'Innovation (art nouveau department store in Brussels)*	•*Anton Chekhov:* The Three Sisters •*Strindberg:* The Dance of Death	•*Rudyard Kipling:* Kim •*Edward Elgar:* Pomp and Circumstance (No. 1)
1902		•*South Africa: second Boer War ends* •*Anglo-Japanese alliance*	•*Carlo Bugatti: Snail Room* •*Burnham: Flatiron Building in New York*	•*George Méliès's A Trip to the Moon: first science fiction film (14 minutes)*	•*Scott Joplin:* "The Entertainer" •*Arthur Conan Doyle:* The Hound of the Baskervilles
1903	•*Deaths of Gauguin and Pissarro* •*Paris: Salon d'Automne founded*	•*Wright brothers complete first powered flight* •*U.K.: Women's Social and Political Union*	•*Mackintosh: Willow Tea Rooms in Glasgow (to 1905)* •*Vienna Workshops organized*	•*Edwin S. Porter's* The Great Train Robbery: *first Western film (11 minutes)*	•*Jack London:* Call of the Wild •*Henry James:* The Ambassadors
1904	•*Picasso moves to Paris* •*Matisse ignites Fauvism with* Luxe, Calme et Volupté	•*Japan and Russia at war (to 1905)* •*U.K. and France: Entente Cordiale*	•*Otto Wagner: modernist Post Office Savings Bank in Vienna (to 1906)*	•*Camille Clifford's stage debut in London* •*Dublin: Abbey Theatre opens*	•*Puccini:* Madame Butterfly •*Joseph Conrad:* Nostromo
1905	•*Paris: first Fauve exhibition* •*Dresden: Expressionist group Die Brücke formed*	•*Norway gains independence from Sweden* •*Russia: first revolution*	•*Antonio Gaudi begins designing Casa Milá (to 1907)*	•*George Bernard Shaw:* Mrs. Warren's Profession •*U.S.: first nickelodeon theaters open*	•*Albert Einstein: Special Theory of Relativity* •*Franz Lehár:* The Merry Widow
1906	•*Derain:* The Pool of London •*Death of Cézanne*	•*U.S.: San Francisco earthquake* •*France: end of Dreyfus Affair (Dreyfus cleared)*	•*McKim, Mead, and White: Pennsylvania Station in New York (to 1910)*	•*Tait brother's* The Story of the Kelly Gang: *first feature film (80 minutes)* •*J. Stuart Blackton: one of the first cartoon films*	•*John Galsworthy:* The Man of Property (first Forsythe Saga *novel*)
1907	•*Klimt:* The Kiss (to 1908) •*Picasso:* Les Demoiselles d'Avignon (first Cubist art)	•*New Zealand acquires Dominion status* •*Russia, U.K., and France: Triple Entente*	•*Munich: Deutsche Werkbund founded* •*P. Behrens starts industrial design for AEG*	•*J. M. Synge:* The Playboy of the Western World •*Ziegfeld Follies opens in New York*	•*Hillaire Belloc:* Cautionary Tales •*Maxim Gorky:* Mother
1908	•*Braque:* Houses at L'Estaque •*Brancusi: early versions of* The Kiss	•*Austria annexes Bosnia-Herzegovina* •*Henry Ford launches Model T car*	•*Behrens: AEG Turbine Factory in Berlin (to 1909)*		•*E. M. Forster:* A Room With a View •*Bartok:* "String Quartet No. 1"
1909	•*Italian writer F. T. Marinetti publishes first Futurist manifesto in French paper* Le Figaro	•*Blériot flies across the English Channel* •*Young Turks overthrow Turkish sultan*	•*Frank Lloyd Wright: Robie House in Chicago*	•*Paris: first performance of the Russian Ballet* •*France: Pathé newsreel introduced*	•*Gustav Mahler:* The Song of the Earth •*Strauss:* Der Rosenkavalier

GLOSSARY

art nouveau: a design style that features plant and flower forms with graceful, curving lines.

avant-garde: having, or pioneering the development of, new, bold, or experimental styles or techniques.

composition: the placement or arrangement of elements, such as shape, color, and balance, in a work of art.

Cubism: a modern art style that features abstract, geometric shapes and fragmented forms.

decadent: in a state of moral decline or decay.

eclectic: made up of a variety of styles, often drawn from diverse sources, that are considered "the best" of their type or class.

Impressionism: a style of painting, especially among French artists in the late 1800s, that depicted everyday objects and scenes with dabs or strokes of color, trying to imitate the fleeting effects of reflected light the way it is seen by the human eye.

perspective: the creation of three-dimensional space and depth on a flat, two-dimensional surface, such as an artist's canvas.

Pointillism: a style of painting, developed in the 1880s, in which the artist, to achieve more vibrant color, applied small strokes or dots of primary colors that would blend together when viewed from a distance.

stylized: represented as an artistic design or pattern, rather than in a natural or traditional form.

Symbolism: an art movement of the late 1800s that rejected the realistic presentation of scenes and objects by using shapes, colors, and symbols to suggest meanings and to portray emotions, dreams, and ideas.

MORE BOOKS TO READ

1900–20: The Birth of Modernism. 20th Century Design (series). Jackie Gaff (Gareth Stevens)

Auguste Rodin. Life and Work of (series). Richard Tames (Heinemann Library)

Cézanne. Famous Artists (series). Antony Mason, Andrew S. Hughes, and Jen Green (Barrons)

Cubism. Art Revolutions (series). Linda Bolton (Peter Bedrick Books)

Impressionist Art. Off the Wall Museum Guides for Kids (series). Ruthie Knapp and Janice Lehmberg (Davis Publications)

Mary Cassatt: Portrait of an American Impressionist. Trailblazers Biographies (series). Thomas Streissguth (Carolrhoda Books)

Matisse. Famous Artists (series). Antony Mason, Andrew S. Hughes, and Jen Green (Barrons)

Perspective. Eyewitness (series). Alison Cole (DK Publishing)

Picasso: Breaking the Rules of Art. Great Artists (series). David Spence (Barrons)

Van Gogh. Eyewitness (series). Bruce Bernard (DK Publishing)

WEB SITES

ArtLex Visual Arts Dictionary: Cubism. *www.artlex.com/ArtLex/c/cubism.html*

The Fauves: The Wild Beasts of Early 20th Century Art. *www.geocities.com/CapeCanaveral/2933/fauves*

Gardens of the Sunlight: The Art of Impressionism. *art.koti.com.pl/index_en.html*

WebMuseum, Paris: Seurat, Georges. *www.ibiblio.org/wm/paint/auth/seurat*

Due to the dynamic nature of the Internet, some web sites stay current longer than others. To find additional web sites, use a reliable search engine with one or more of the following keywords: *art nouveau, Cubism, Die Brücke, Expressionism, Fauvism, Impressionism, Pointillism, Symbolism,* and the names of individual artists.

INDEX